The Lost Horizon
by Captain Chris Couch

$$\text{Tan } L2 \times \text{Sin } DLO1 = \text{Tan } L1 \times \text{Sin } SLO2$$
$$\text{Sin } DLO12$$

The Vanishing Art of Navigation

A Spirits Journey to Where We Began

Copyright © 2012 Compass Headings Publishing.
All rights reserved. Printed and bound in the United States of America.
No part of this book may be used or reproduced or transmitted
in any manner whatsoever—except brief passages for the specific purpose
of review or promotion—without written permission from the publisher.

For information, please contact
Compass Headings Publishing, 9805 NE 116th #7231, Kirkland, WA 98034.

First Edition
_____

ISBN 0982941528
_____

We welcome comments, suggestions
or corrections for possible use in future editions.

Write to us:
Compass Headings Publishing,
9805 NE 116th #7231, Kirkland, WA 98034.

captaincouch@earthlink.net

Photography by istockphoto.com
The following photos by Chris Couch:

The Lost Horizon
The Vanishing Art of Navigation
By Captain Chris Couch

Contents

The History of Navigation 5
Where It All Starts 7
Piloting 9
The Magnetic Compass 11
The Navigational Fix 12
The Visual Fix 13
The Radar Fix 13
Celestial Navigation Theory 14
The Navigational Triangle 16
The Altitude Intercept Method 19
What you will need: 20
Sextant Adjustment 23
Latitude By Polaris 28
Latitude by LAN 30
Local Apparent Noon LAN 32
Sun Line 34
The Moon, Planets and Stars 37
Great Circle Calculator 41

Forward

I consider myself very fortunate to have spent the first part of my marine career in the time before GPS and computers. When I first started to navigate ships, I used Visual Bearings, Analog Radar, Radio Beacons, Loran A, Omega and the Transit Satellite System. And yes, Celestial Navigation.

In my years in the Coast Guard we positioned all navigational buoys using the marine sextant and terrestrial horizontal angles. We used celestial fixes to position offshore weather and research buoys.

Just in my lifetime, we have gone from the simple radio direction finder to GPS. From large clumsey paper charts to chart plotters to having it all on your iPhone.

The "Art" of Navigation has all but been rendered obsolete.

The History of Navigation

Since it was first published in 1802, the American Practical Navigator by Nathaniel Bowditch has been the leading navigational text and reference.

This is the must have book for any person who has an interest in Marine Navigation and it's history. I highly recommend it.

American Practical Navigator Volume I. By Nathaniel Bowditch.

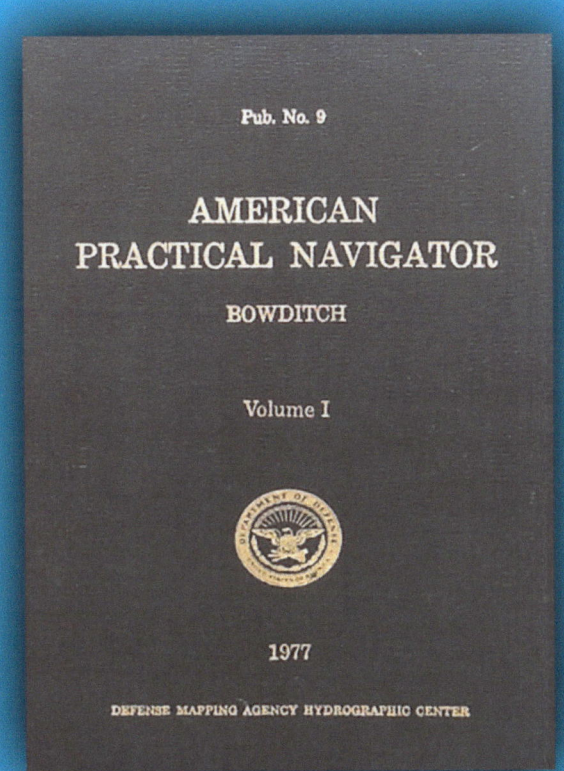

Light Show
by Chris Couch

Rocking gently
In a following sea
A warm moist breeze
Blows gently past me

Looking back
As my world slowly spins
This day is setting
Somewhere, a new one begins

My mind fills quickly
with dreams full of stars
How do you describe
This place in which we are

A spirits glittered trail
Brightens the truth
Against the darkened skies
Oh, the things I have seen
With these eyes

Alone I stand
Sound of the water
The smell of the sea
Her light show
That surrounds me

This moment washes softly
Across my face
As her thoughts wet my lips
It is the sea that I taste

Where It All Starts

In the beginning, from the time man started his travels upon this planet, he observed and made note of his surroundings to aid him in his journey. From the Polynesians who observed the prevailing winds, currents, swells and night sky to aid them in their transpacific voyages to the ancient Norsemen who also used bird and whale migrations.

The early first mariners were master observers of their environment. The first elements of navigation as we know it probably started in the Mediterranean with trade between emerging civilizations. The lighthouse and many shore based visual aids to navigation owe their beginnings to this area.

One of the earliest well recorded voyages was by a Greek astronomer and navigator known as Pytheas. Sometime between the years 350 and 300 BC, he sailed from a Mediterranean port to England and then on to Scotland, the Norwegian fiords and northwest Germany.

What makes this so significant is that Pytheas and others of the time accomplished this with no compass, no sextant and no timepieces.

Although basic piloting along the coastline was used, there would have been many times these ancient mariners would have been out of sight of land.

This is where their unique observations of the winds, seas and stars came into play to get them safely back to port.

The Presence
by Chris Couch

Time sets to a place
Where shimmered metallic colors collide
The feelings I have
When I am in your presence
Only tears
Are able to describe

As all traces
Begin to slowly disappear
And my world goes completely blind
The rolling nudges
Of your gentle touch
Is all that is left behind

Wrapped in your darkness
With only my dreams
To light the way
Thoughts of you
Sparkle in the distance
As your spirits
Come out to play

Alone again
In your midst
Upon waters so dark and blue
I ask you again to watch over me
And place my faith
In you

And now as twilight stirs me
From places I have never been
A new days journey has started
Humbled in your presence
Once again

Piloting

The practice of visual observation to fix your position and follow your your intended route is called Piloting and still remains today the fundamental basis of navigation.

Piloting is the practice of correlating what you see "around you" with what you see "on your chart".

You then use this observation and correlation to fix and continually monitor your approximate position relative to the chart and safe water.

With today's technology however, I see too many starring down at their chart plotters and not looking outside and observing the world around them.

Practice identifying the buoys, lights and landmarks that you see with what is on your chart and with your radar.

The more you do this, the more proficient as a mariner and navigator you will become.

Our Secret
by Chris Couch

Alone on an open sea
Gazing at a star filled sky
Where would I be?
Had I passed this planet by

An empty vessel
Floating through time and space
A blue marbled port
How on earth did I land in this place?

Not easy is this world
A life of battles
Defeats and victories hard fought
Seeking balance on the surface
While living deep in thought

An unknown destination
Towards which I ride
Beyond a moonlit horizon
Where my two worlds collide

A truth we have learned
This secret we share
Feeling her movement
Breathing her air

Taking measure of life
Standing at the edge of this step
All I have lost
All I have kept

Having forgotten more
Than most will learn
Surrounded in her cold darkness
She beckons for my return

The Magnetic Compass

A needle thrust through a straw and floated in a container of water is what describes the earliest "known" compass. When the magnetic compass was first used is unknown and there is very little to substantiate where it first came from although a widely held belief is that it came from the Chinese around one thousand A.D.

The magnetic north pole of our planet is a feature of Earth's electromagnetic field.

This field is produced by our spinning molten core and literally deflects incoming cosmic radiation protecting life at the surface. The spectacular northern lights is the result of solar particles reacting to the upper atmosphere and illuminating these electromagnetic lines of force.

The Magnetic Compass is our only non-electronic instrument we have to maintain directional orientation. The magnetic variation we find listed on our charts is the difference between true north and magnetic north. Because of the moving north pole, fluctuations in the field itself, local disturbances and anomalies, the magnetic compass is also inherently inaccurate. The installation and location of the compass on your vessel will also introduce inaccuracies called Deviation.

Even with all of this, your Magnetic Compass remains the one instrument you can rely on when all else fails.

The Navigational Fix

By definition, a fix is the intersection of at least three **lines of position (LOP)**.

A *line of position* can be a bearing to a charted object, a radar range to a point of land or the beach. In loran C it is the time difference between a master and slave transmitting stations and with GPS the time the signal takes to travel from the satellite to your receiver.

A line of position using the sun, moon, plants or stars is no different. The angle between a body and the horizon translates into a line of equal altitude which if plotted on the globe would look like a circle. The circle of equal altitude. This is our line of position.

The Dead Reckon

Dead Reckoning was undoubtedly used the first time the earliest mariners sailed beyond the sight of land. It is a way to predict your approximate position into the future using your heading steered, estimated speed and time. It was the only way of monitoring your vessels progress and position between land falls and celestial observations.

From the first voyage ever taken until the mid 1960's when Omega and Loran A became widely used, Dead Reckoning was an essential part of Navigation.

Today a mental projection of where you will be and when, is still necessary for proper trip planning, weather forecasts, tide and current conditions.

Think ahead. Plan ahead.

The Visual Fix

1. Visually correlate two to three objects that are plotted on your chart. Tank, spire, lighthouse, tower, cupola, etc., anything that you can see that is also plotted on the chart.

2. With your compass equipped device (binoculars, handheld pelorus) take the Magnetic bearing to that object.

3. With your parallel plotter, align the plotter with magnetic bearing on the Compass Rose on your chart.

4. Slide your plotter to the charted object and draw the reciprocal bearing line.

5. This is your line of position. Repeat for the next object.

6. Where these lines of position cross is your position or fix.

The Radar Fix

1. On your Radar screen, correlate two to three radar returns with those on your chart. Any land feature or fixed structure that can be identified on the chart.

2. Measure the distance to that feature on the radar.

3. Using a compass and the latitude scale or distance scale of the chart, mark the distance.

4. Putting the point of your compass on the charted feature, scribe an arc.

5. This is your line of position. Repeat for the next feature.

6. Where these arcs cross is your position or fix.

A combination of visual bearings and radar ranges may be used.

Celestial Navigation Theory

As someone who taught himself celestial navigation, I know all too well how complicated it can appear on the surface.

As someone who enjoys teaching however, I will show you how simple and understandable celestial navigation really is.

At any moment in time, any celestial body (sun, moon, planets, stars) is directly overhead somewhere on the earth. Let's use the sun.

At any moment in time, the Sun is directly overhead (90 degrees) somewhere on the face of the planet.

This spot is called its geographic position. This position can be described by the suns declination (Latitude) and by its Greenwich Hour Angle (GHA) (Longitude).

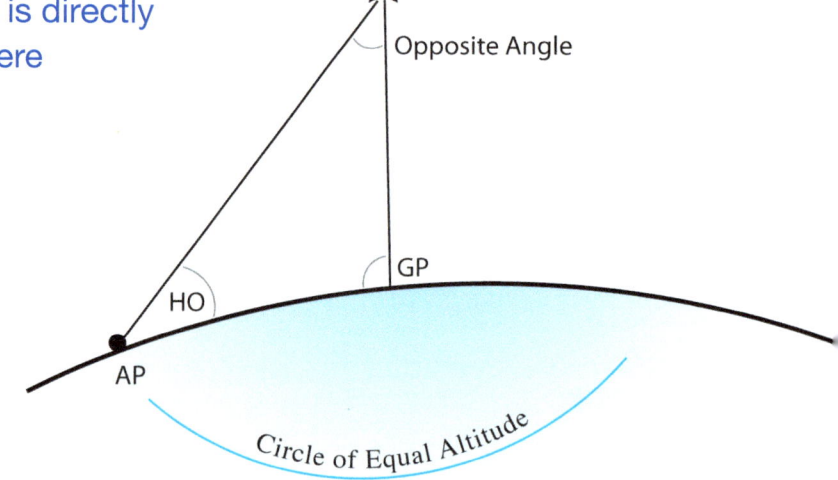

If we were standing directly under the sun at that moment when it was 90 degrees overhead, that would be our position.

Declination is the position of the Sun North or South of the Equator and equates to Latitude. The Earth is tilted on its axis at 23.5 deg. As it orbits the sun it causes the suns geographic position to move north and south. It is at its furthest north the first day of summer and furthest South the first day of winter.

Greenwich Hour Angle (GHA) is the Suns position West of Greenwich and equates to Longitude.

    1 Deg of Arc/Latitude is equal to 60 nm.
    1 Min of Arc/Latitude is equal to 1 nm.

    1 Dec of Arc/Longitude is equal to 4 min of time.
        Conversion of Arc to time is in the Nautical Almanac
        and is used in determining time of Local Apparent Noon.

Now, let's step back from that spot, let's say a mile. We take our sextant and observe the angle between the sun and the horizon. 89 degrees 59 minutes 0 seconds.

Relative to us, the sun has moved one minute of arc. The circle of equal altitude we are standing on is one mile from the suns geographic position.

In reality however, it is unlikely we would happen to be so close to a bodies geographic position. Let's say our observation of the sun was 50 degrees. The opposite angle would be 40 degrees.
40 times 60 is 2400. The semi diameter of our circle of Equal altitude would be 2400 nautical miles!

How could we possibly plot that on a chart?

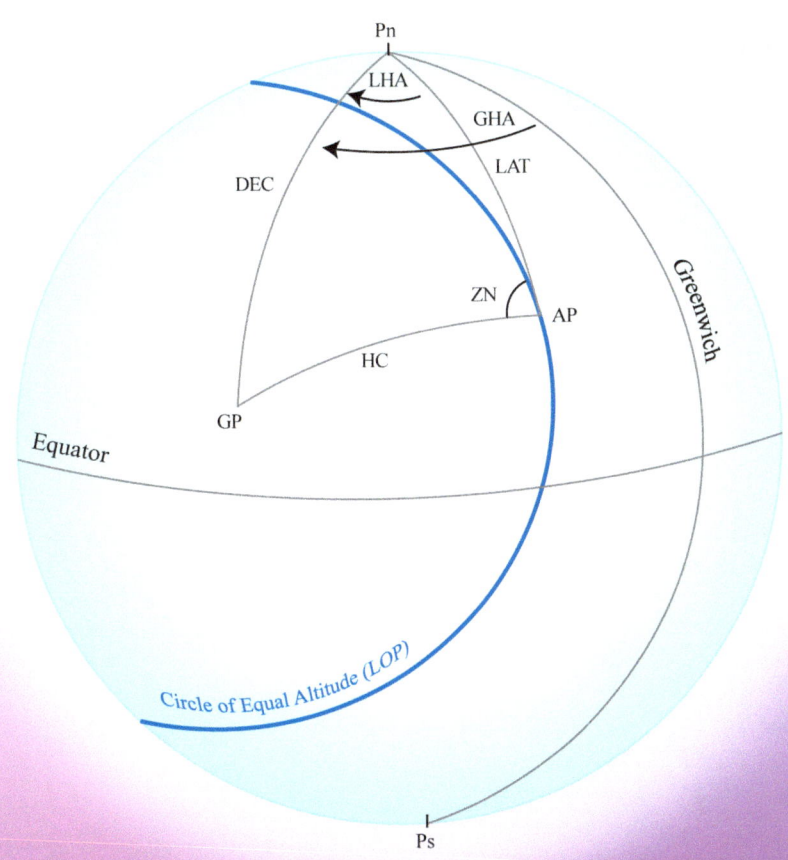

The Navigational Triangle

In a flat plane triangle, when two sides and one angle (SAS) are known, with trigonometry, the third side and remaining angles can be solved.

Because we are laying this triangle over the globe, it now becomes a spherical trigonometry solution.

The two sides we know are our assumed Latitude and the suns Declination. The angle we know is the angle between our Assumed Position and the suns GHA called the Local Hour Angle LHA.

The Solution

When we enter Pub 229, the Sight Reduction Tables with our Latitude Suns Declination and Local Hour Angle, we solve for the third leg of the triangle which is the computed altitude of the Sun (HC) and the second angle which is the bearing or Azimuth (Az) to the Sun.

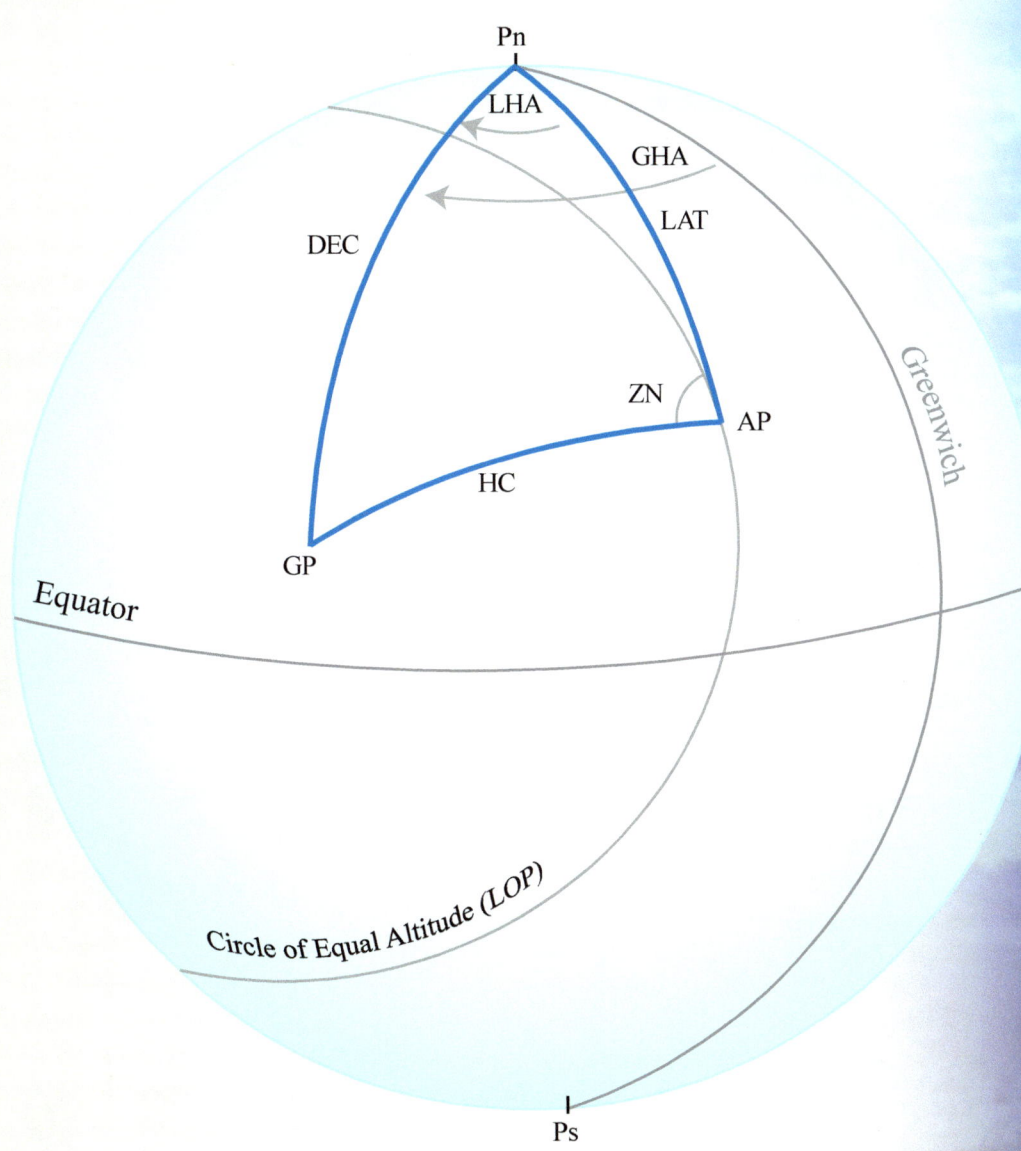

AP Your Approximate Position.
GP Objects Geographical Position. Declination and GHA
HC Height Computed. Taken from Pub 229
Zn Azimuth or bearing to the object. Taken from Pub 229

Pub 229 Entering Arguments:

LHA. Local Hour Angle. Angle between your Long and objects GHA.
LHA = GHA - W Long or + E Long
Note: Long is changed to make LHA a whole number
New Lat and Long become AP.

Latitude This is your DR Lat rounded to nearest whole Lat.

Dec Declination. Taken from Nautical Almanac.
Exact Dec for time of observation.

Where
by Chris Couch

Where do I go
When I sail off to shores
Never been?
How will I get there?
As she rocks me gently
Once again

Why have I sacrificed
So much to be alone?
In this place that feels
So much
Like home

Everytime
She reaches into me
How do I learn to listen
How do I learn to see

The visions she shows
With each swell
That rolls by
I know I belong
But I don't know why

What is wrong?
And who is right?
Why am I here?
I ask of her
Each night

Where it all started
Life that blows in the wind
Where will I go?
When this all
Comes to an end

The Altitude Intercept Method

Four hundred years ago, a navigator named Pedro Nunes using observed altitudes of the sun plotted the circles of equal altitude on a globe to fix his position.

In 1837, the thirty year old ships captain Thomas Sumner produced the celestial line of position followed later by Marcq St.-Hilaire who gave us the Altitude Intercept Method. A way of plotting a small section of the circle of equal altitude on a navigational chart.

Using our assumed position (AP) as a starting point. We are plotting the bearing to the body and then the difference between height computed and height observed. This becomes our line of position.

Computed Greater Away

If height computed HC is greater than height observed HO, then the difference is plotted away or opposite direction of the azimuth to the object.

Summary of Altitude Intercept Method

Plot AP - Lat to nearest whole Lat. Long used for GHA.

Draw bearing/azimuth to or from the object. Computed greater away.

Mark difference between Height computed and observed in nautical miles.

Draw line perpendicular to bearing.

This is your LOP.

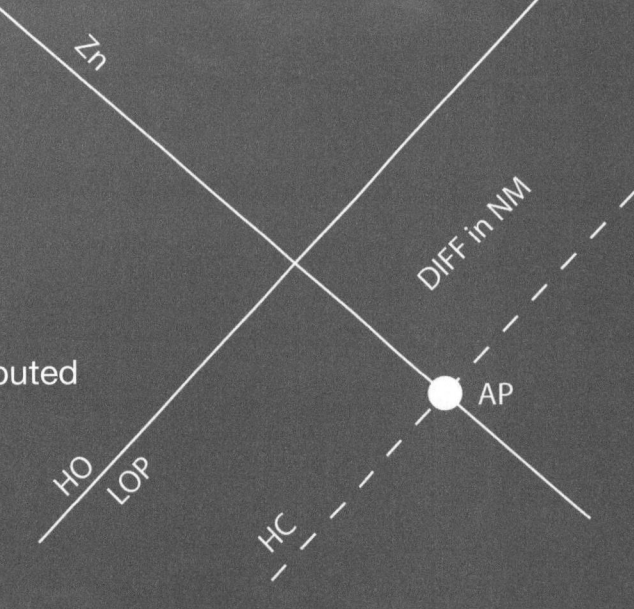

What you will need:
- Marine Sextant
- Timepiece (accurate to the second)
- H.O. Pub No. 229 Volumes 1 through 4. Sight Reduction Tables
- Nautical Almanac
- Universal Plotting Sheets
- Weems and Plath Parallel Plotter
- Dividers
- Pencil

The Nautical Almanac

The Nautical Almanac contains hourly GHA Greenwich Hour Angle and Dec Declination for the Sun, Moon, Aries, Venus, Mars, Jupiter and Saturn.

In addition, it also lists SHA Sidereal Hour Angle and Dec Declination for selected navigational Stars. Altitude Correction Tables for the Sun, Stars and Planets.

A Separate Altitude Correction Table for the Moon and tables for Polaris.

Publication 229

The six-volume series of the Sight Reduction Tables for Marine Navigation contains the tables designed to solve the navigational triangle.

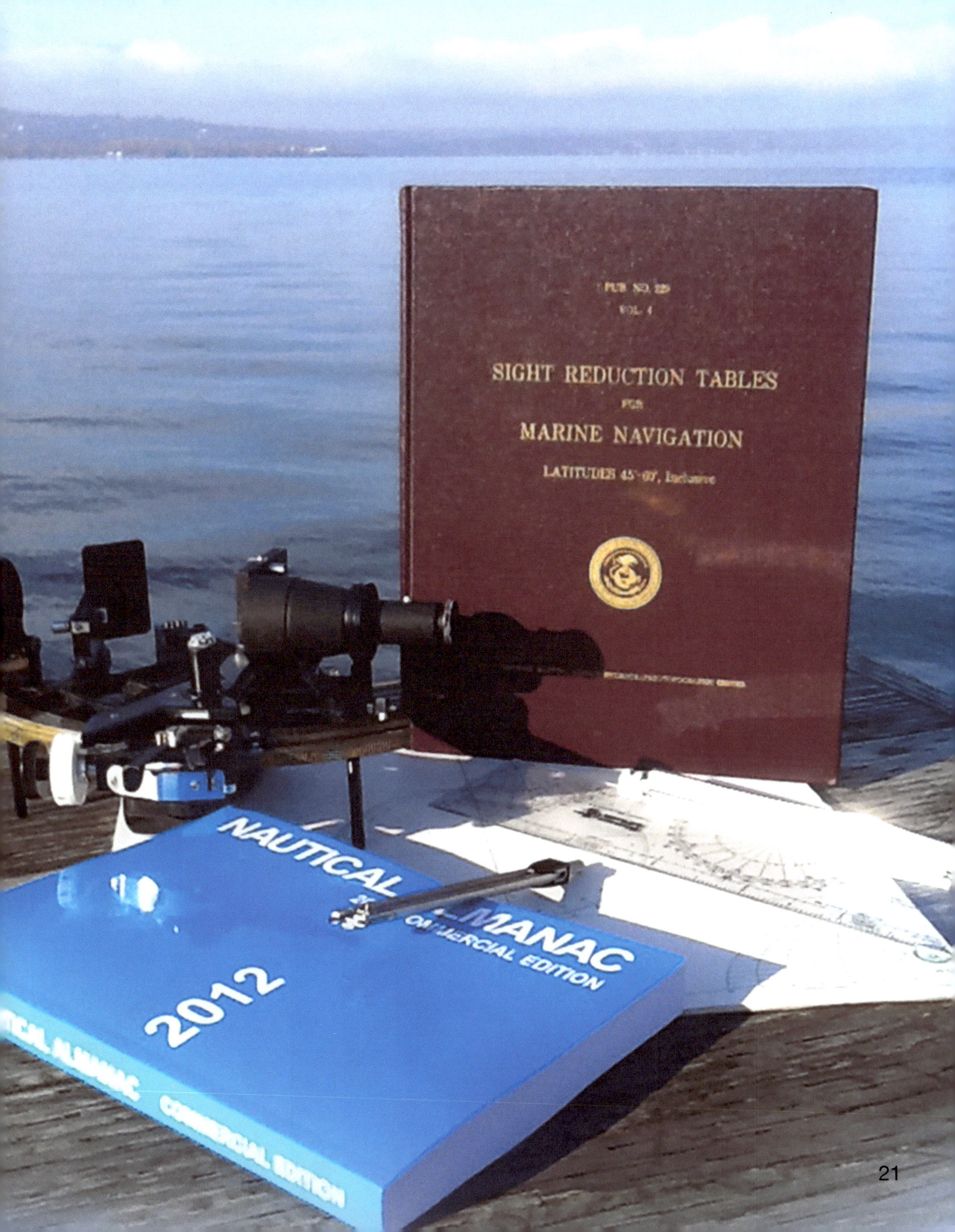
SIGHT REDUCTION TABLES
FOR
MARINE NAVIGATION
NAUTICAL ALMANAC
COMMERCIAL EDITION
2012

The Marine Sextant

Sextant Adjustment

Your marine sextant measures the angle between two objects in degrees, minutes and seconds. 60 seconds to minute, 60 minutes to a degree.
An error of only one minute of arc can throw your line of position Off by a mile. Properly adjusting your sextant is crucial.
Sextant Adjustment steps/photos

There are three adjustments to be checked and/or made.

1. The Index Mirror perpendicular to the Frame.
   A. Move Index Arm to approximately 35 degrees.
   B. Holding the Sextant backwards with the Arc away from you, sight the Arc and the reflected part of the Arc in the Index Mirror.
   C. Now adjust the Index Mirror until the two images are aligned.
   D. The Index Mirror is now perpendicular to the Frame.

2. The Horizon Glass parallel to the Index Mirror.
   A. Set the Index Arm and Micrometer Drum to zero.
   B. Holding the Sextant vertically, sight on a far away horizontal structure or a clear horizon. Note the real and reflected images.
   C. Using the upper adjustment screw on the Horizon Glass, adjust until the images become one or continuous.
   D. The Horizon Glass is now parallel to the Index Mirror.

3. The Horizon Glass perpendicular to the Frame.
   A. Keep the Index Arm and Micrometer Drum set to zero.
   B. Sight on the same horizontal structure as before.
   C. Now rotate the sextant 45 degrees to the right and note the image. Rotate 45 degrees to the left and note the image.
   D. Using the lower left adjustment screw on the Horizon Glass, adjust until the image is one or continuous.
   E. The Horizon Glass is now perpendicular to the Frame

Reflect *by Chris Couch*

Tears shimmer
Off mirrored surfaced seas
A soft breeze whispers
Then brings me to my knees

Spirits that swim deep
Those who own the skies
The way I feel
Seeing you in my eyes

A journey on this ocean
That has been my home
Surrounded by so much
Having never felt
So alone

The voice I hear
With each wave that dies
The truth I face
Behind me
Only lies

Taken by the hand
Through this uncertain world
Guiding my sails
Through your swells
Softly curled

All that is me
I struggle to keep
Lost in this reflected moment
On your waters
So deep

The Observation

What body will be observed?
Sun, Moon, Polaris, Planets or Star?

What type of sighting will this be?

Sun Line, Lat by LAN or Polaris.

Have sextant, watch, pencil and paper at the ready.

1. Bring object and horizon into view.

2. Rotate sextant to swing object through horizon.

3. Adjust until lower limb of object is sitting on the horizon. For a star put center of the body on the horizon.

4. Immediately note and record the time. Hours, minutes and seconds GMT

5. Record the sextant reading. Degrees, minutes and seconds in tenths.

Sextant Altitude Corrections

The angle we observe between the celestial body and the visible horizon HS or height shot, must be corrected for a number of factors.

Dip or height of eye. Found in the Altitude Corrections Table in the front of the Nautical Almanac. It is the difference between the horizontal reference plane and the visible horizon. It is always subtracted.

HS minus Dip (height of eye) gives us HA or apparent altitude.

We now apply the Altitude Corrections which include:

Refraction: Correction for the bending of light through the atmosphere.

Semi-Diameter: Correction for 1/2 of the bodies diameter.

Augmentation: Increase in apparent size of the the sun and moon as a result of the increase of apparent altitude.

Parallax: The difference in apparent altitude as viewed from the surface of the earth and the center of the earth.

Additional Corrections: Corrections for barometric pressure and temperature.

HA plus Altitude Corrections (added for lower limb) and plus/minus Additional Corrections gives us HO or Height Observed.

To summarize:

1. HS height shot minus Dip height of eye = HA apparent altitude.

2. HA apparent altitude plus Altitude Corrections and plus or minus Additional Corrections gives us HO height observed.

Note: For the Moon, Altitude Corrections for the Moon is in the back of the Nautical Almanac and is done in two parts and always added.

(page from nautical almanac)

A2 ALTITUDE CORRECTION TABLES 10°-90°—SUN, STARS, PLANETS

OCT.–MAR. SUN APR.–SEPT.				STARS AND PLANETS		DIP				
App. Alt.	Lower Limb	Upper Limb	App. Alt.	Lower Limb	Upper Limb	App. Alt.	Corr^n	App. Alt.	Additional Corr^n	Ht. of Eye	Corr^n	Ht. of Eye	Ht. of Eye	Corr^n

OCT.–MAR. SUN		APR.–SEPT.		STARS AND PLANETS		DIP			
App. Alt.	Lower / Upper Limb	App. Alt.	Lower / Upper Limb	App. Alt.	Corr^n	App. Alt. / Additional Corr^n	Ht. of Eye (m) / Corr^n	Ht. of Eye (ft)	Ht. of Eye (m) / Corr^n
9 33	+10·8 −21·5	9 39	+10·6 −21·2	9 55	−5·3	**2012 VENUS**	2·4 −2·8	8·0	1·0 −1·8
9 45	+10·9 −21·4	9 50	+10·7 −21·1	10 07	−5·2	Jan. 1–Feb. 20	2·6 −2·9	8·6	1·5 −2·2
9 56	+11·0 −21·3	10 02	+10·8 −21·0	10 20	−5·1	Sept. 20–Dec. 31	2·8 −3·0	9·2	2·0 −2·5
10 08	+11·1 −21·2	10 14	+10·9 −20·9	10 32	−5·0		3·0 −3·1	9·8	2·5 −2·8
10 20	+11·2 −21·1	10 27	+11·0 −20·8	10 46	−4·9	0 ′	3·2 −3·2	10·5	3·0 −3·0
10 33	+11·3 −21·0	10 40	+11·1 −20·7	10 59	−4·8	60 +0·1	3·4 −3·3	11·2	See table ←
10 46	+11·4 −20·9	10 53	+11·2 −20·6	11 14	−4·7	Feb. 21–Apr. 12	3·6 −3·4	11·9	
11 00	+11·5 −20·8	11 07	+11·3 −20·5	11 29	−4·6	July 31–Sept. 19	3·8 −3·5	12·6	m ′
11 15	+11·6 −20·7	11 22	+11·4 −20·4	11 44	−4·5		4·0 −3·6	13·3	20 −7·9
11 30	+11·7 −20·6	11 37	+11·5 −20·3	12 00	−4·4	0 ′	4·3 −3·7	14·1	22 −8·3
11 45	+11·8 −20·5	11 53	+11·6 −20·2	12 17	−4·3	41 +0·2	4·5 −3·8	14·9	24 −8·6
12 01	+11·9 −20·4	12 10	+11·7 −20·1	12 35	−4·2	76 +0·1	4·7 −3·9	15·7	26 −9·0
12 18	+12·0 −20·3	12 27	+11·8 −20·0	12 53	−4·1	Apr. 13–May 4	5·0 −4·0	16·5	28 −9·3
12 36	+12·1 −20·2	12 45	+11·9 −19·9	13 12	−4·0	July 9–July 30	5·2 −4·1	17·4	
12 54	+12·2 −20·1	13 04	+12·0 −19·8	13 32	−3·9		5·5 −4·2	18·3	30 −9·6
13 14	+12·3 −20·0	13 24	+12·1 −19·7	13 53	−3·8	0 ′	5·8 −4·3	19·1	32 −10·0
13 34	+12·4 −19·9	13 44	+12·2 −19·6	14 16	−3·7	34 +0·3	6·1 −4·4	20·1	34 −10·3
13 55	+12·5 −19·8	14 06	+12·3 −19·5	14 39	−3·6	60 +0·2	6·3 −4·5	21·0	36 −10·6
14 17	+12·6 −19·7	14 29	+12·4 −19·4	15 03	−3·5	80 +0·1	6·6 −4·6	22·0	38 −10·8
14 41	+12·7 −19·6	14 53	+12·5 −19·3	15 29	−3·4	May 5–May 21	6·9 −4·7	22·9	
15 05	+12·8 −19·5	15 18	+12·6 −19·2	15 56	−3·3	June 22–July 8	7·2 −4·8	23·9	40 −11·1
15 31	+12·9 −19·4	15 45	+12·7 −19·1	16 25	−3·2		7·5 −4·9	24·9	42 −11·4
15 59	+13·0 −19·3	16 13	+12·8 −19·0	16 55	−3·1	0 ′	7·9 −5·0	26·0	44 −11·7
16 27	+13·1 −19·2	16 43	+12·9 −18·9	17 27	−3·0	29 +0·4	8·2 −5·1	27·1	46 −11·9
16 58	+13·2 −19·1	17 14	+13·0 −18·8	18 01	−2·9	51 +0·3	8·5 −5·2	28·1	48 −12·2
17 30	+13·3 −19·0	17 47	+13·1 −18·7	18 37	−2·8	68 +0·2	8·8 −5·3	29·2	
18 05	+13·4 −18·9	18 23	+13·2 −18·6	19 16	−2·7	83 +0·1	9·2 −5·4	30·4	ft. ′
18 41	+13·5 −18·8	19 00	+13·3 −18·5	19 56	−2·6	May 22–June 21	9·5 −5·5	31·5	2 −1·4
19 20	+13·6 −18·7	19 41	+13·4 −18·4	20 40	−2·5		9·9 −5·6	32·7	4 −1·9
20 02	+13·7 −18·6	20 24	+13·5 −18·3	21 27	−2·4	0 ′	10·3 −5·7	33·9	6 −2·4
20 46	+13·8 −18·5	21 10	+13·6 −18·2	22 17	−2·3	26 +0·5	10·6 −5·8	35·1	8 −2·7
21 34	+13·9 −18·4	21 59	+13·7 −18·1	23 11	−2·2	46 +0·4	11·0 −5·9	36·3	10 −3·1
22 25	+14·0 −18·3	22 52	+13·8 −18·0	24 09	−2·1	60 +0·3	11·4 −6·0	37·6	See table ←
23 20	+14·1 −18·2	23 49	+13·9 −17·9	25 12	−2·0	73 +0·2	11·8 −6·1	38·9	
24 20	+14·2 −18·1	24 51	+14·0 −17·8	26 20	−1·9	84 +0·1	12·2 −6·2	40·1	ft. ′
25 24	+14·3 −18·0	25 58	+14·1 −17·7	27 34	−1·8	**MARS**	12·6 −6·3	41·5	70 −8·1
26 34	+14·4 −17·9	27 11	+14·2 −17·6	28 54	−1·7	Jan. 1–Jan. 8	13·0 −6·4	42·8	75 −8·4
27 50	+14·5 −17·8	28 31	+14·3 −17·5	30 22	−1·6	May 6–Dec. 31	13·4 −6·5	44·2	80 −8·7
29 13	+14·6 −17·7	29 58	+14·4 −17·4	31 58	−1·5		13·8 −6·6	45·5	85 −8·9
30 44	+14·7 −17·6	31 33	+14·5 −17·3	33 43	−1·4	0 ′	14·2 −6·7	46·9	90 −9·2
32 24	+14·8 −17·5	33 18	+14·6 −17·2	35 38	−1·3	60 +0·1	14·7 −6·8	48·4	95 −9·5
34 15	+14·9 −17·4	35 15	+14·7 −17·1	37 45	−1·2	Jan. 9–May 5	15·1 −6·9	49·8	
36 17	+15·0 −17·3	37 24	+14·8 −17·0	40 06	−1·1		15·5 −7·0	51·3	100 −9·7
38 34	+15·1 −17·2	39 48	+14·9 −16·9	42 42	−1·0	0 ′	16·0 −7·1	52·8	105 −9·9
41 06	+15·2 −17·1	42 28	+15·0 −16·8	45 34	−0·9	41 +0·2	16·5 −7·2	54·3	110 −10·2
43 56	+15·3 −17·0	45 29	+15·1 −16·7	48 45	−0·8	76 +0·1	16·9 −7·3	55·8	115 −10·4
47 07	+15·4 −16·9	48 52	+15·2 −16·6	52 16	−0·7		17·4 −7·4	57·4	120 −10·6
							17·9	58·9	125 −10·8

Latitude By Polaris

Because of its fixed position in the sky, Polaris was probably the first star used for marine navigation.

When the pole star was first used to determine latitude is not known.

By the time of Columbus some navigators where using it and with the advent of a specialized instrument called the Nocturnal in the late 1500's it became more widespread.

Because Polaris happens to sit directly above the geographical North Pole, the Height Observed is also your Latitude.

Worksheet
Latitude by Polaris

Date	
DR Lat	
DR Long	

Make Observation	
Tab GHA Aries	
Incr'mts Aries	
GHA of Aries	
DR Long	
Exact LHA of Aries	

Hs	
Dip (ht of eye)	
Alt Corr.	
Temp/Baro (Ha<10)	
a0 +	
a1 +	
a2 +	
Total Corr.	
Ha	
Subtract 60.0'	
Latitude	

Make observation

Record time

Calculate exact LHA of Aries

   (Nautical Almanac)

LHA Aries = GHA Aries - Wlong +Elong

Correct Height Shot for

Dip and Altitude Corrections

Enter Polaris Tables

   (Nautical Almanac)

Add corrections

Subtract 60.0 min

To arrive at your Latitude

Latitude by LAN

The ability to determine Latitude at sea has been around for thousands of years.

Since before the Christian era, astronomers had used daily observations to calculate the suns declination (dec) and then produce the tables containing that information.

It wasn't until the 15th century though that experienced seamen where determining their Latitude at sea to within a few degrees.

Until the advent of accurate time at sea and a way of determining longitude, the practice of parallel sailing was common. On ocean crossings, ships would sail north or south until the desired Latitude was found, then east or west to their destination.

It wouldn't be until the late 1700's that an accurate timepiece would be available for shipboard use and subsequently more accurate point to point navigation possible.

When the sun is at your local apparent noon, at it's zenith, it is due south or 180 deg true from your position. At that moment all of the components of the navigational triangle exist on the same line or your meridian.

The line of position which is perpendicular to the azimuth to the sun is also your Latitude.

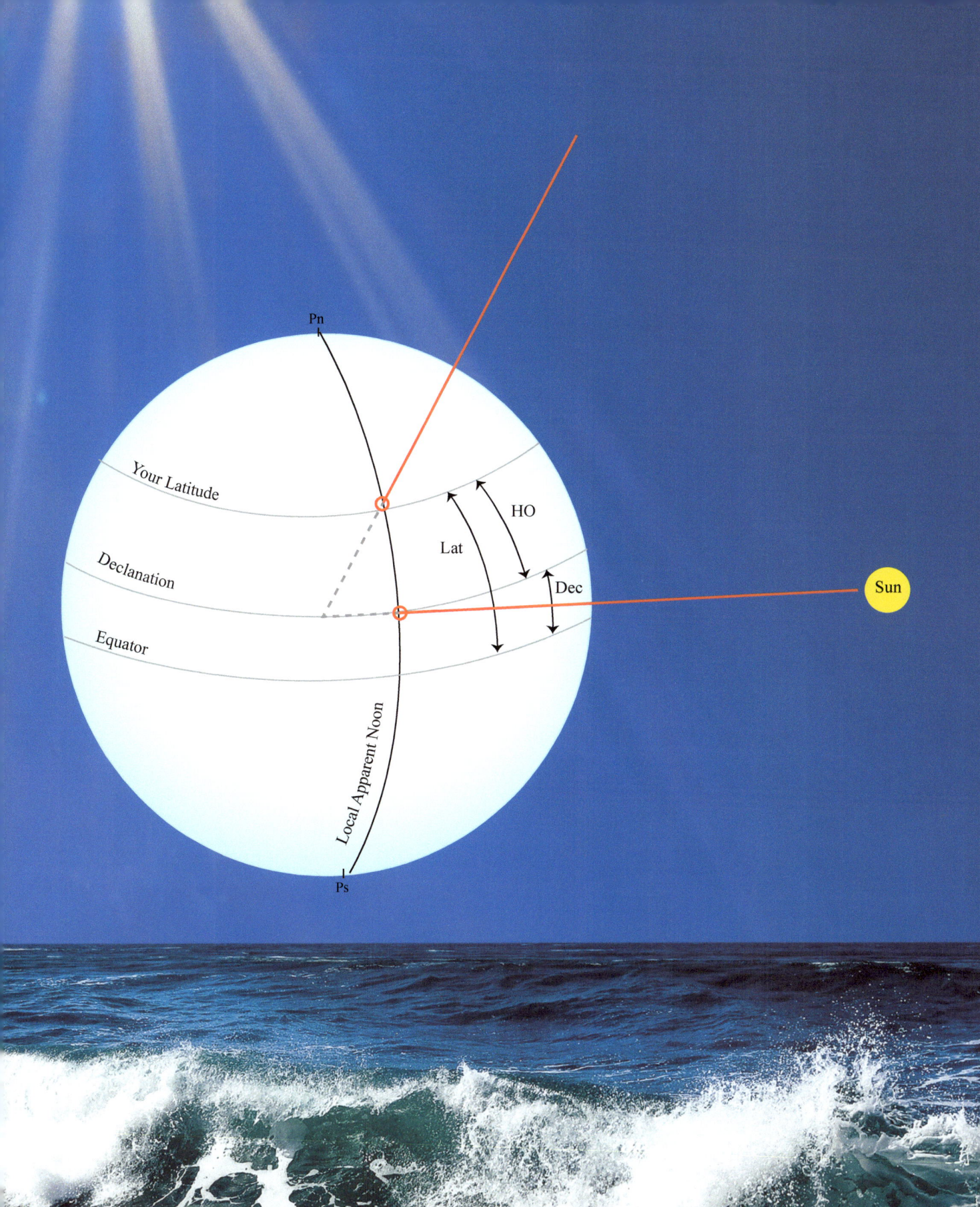

Local Apparent Noon LAN

Your local apparent noon is that moment when the sun passes due south of your position and is at its zenith as it arcs through the sky.

Using the suns altitude ho and declination at that moment gives us our latitude to observe the sun as it reaches LAN we also need to know the time Of LAN

We rotate the 360 degrees of our globe every 24 hours. The sun appears to move across the sky 15 deg every hour.

The 24 time zones of our planet are roughly centered on meridians or lines of longitude every 15 deg.

1. Determine your meridian. 15, 30, 45, 60, 75, 90, 105, 120 etc..

2. Determine the difference in Longitude (arc) east or west of that meridian.

3. Convert arc to time. Nautical Almanac.

4. Determine time of meridian passage from daily pages of Nautical Almanac.
   a. Add or subtract equation of time from mean time of meridian passage.

5. Add or subtract your difference in time to determine time of LAN for your position.

Worksheet Local Apparent Noon Lan

Date	
DR Lat	
DR Long	
Your Meridian	
Diff Long Arc	
Arc to Time	
Eqn of Time	
Time of LAN	

Make Observation	

Begin making observations 10 min Prior to estimated time of LAN

Tab Dec	
d +/-	
d corr.	
True Dec	

Record every minute to catch Sun at top of its arc.

Calculate true Declination (Nautical Almanac)

Hs	
Dip (ht of eye)	
Alt. Corr.	
89-60.0	
Ho	
Zenith Distance	
True Dec.	
Lattitude	

Correct Height shot for Dip and Altitude Corrections

Subtract from 90 deg. (89-60.0)

To arrive at Zenith Distance
If Zdist & Dec are same — Add
If Zdist & Dec are contrary — Subtract

To arrive at your Latitude

Body	
IC	
Dip (ht)	
Hs	
Ha	
Alt. Corr	
Temp/Baro	
H.P. (Moon)	
Ho	

DR Lat	
Lat	

Date	
Obs Time	
GMT	

Tab GHA	
v	
GHA incr'mt	
v corr.	
GHA DR Long	
LHA	

Sun Line

Make observation
Record time

Correct Height Shot for
Dip and Altitude Corrections
To arrive at Height Observed

Pub 229 entering argument
Round DR Lat to nearest
Whole Latitude

Pub 229 entering argument
 (Nautical Almanac)
Determine LHA
LHA = GHA - Wlong or + Elong
Change DR Long so that a whole
Number for LHA will result.

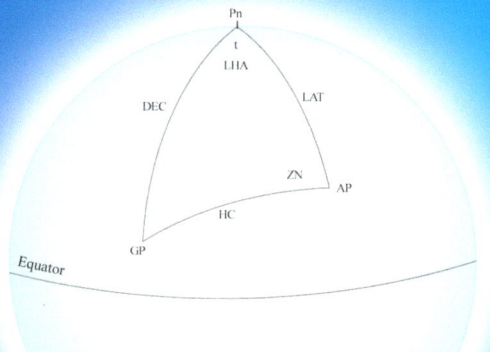

Tab Dec	
d	
d corr+or-	
True Dec	

Pub 229 entering argument
 (Nautical Almanac)
Determine True Declination

Enter Pub 229	
Hc (Tab Alt)	
Dec inc. +/- d	
Tens	
Units	
Total Corr +/-	
Hc (Comp Alt)	
Ho (Obs Alt)	
a (intercept)	
Z	
Zn (Deg True)	
Plot using Altitude Intercept method.	

Enter Pub 229
with LHA, Lat and Dec

Extract HC Height Computed,
d and Z

Using Dec increments and Altitude
Difference d, pull Altitude Correction
From Interpolation Tables in front
And back of 229.

Calculate difference between
HC and HO In nautical miles

Convert Z to Zn.

Plot using Altitude Intercept method
Note: Computed Greater Away

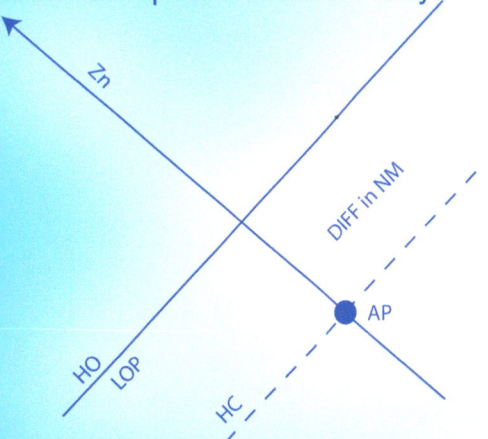

Deep Blue
by Chris Couch

Night fades, morning dawns
With lights gentle stream
I awaken to find myself
Living in the dream

Looking back at a life
I have left behind
Sailing towards a world
That waits on the other side

Breaking the bonds of an earthly grip
As I begin to float free
Enveloped in this state I have become
Alone on an open sea

Surrounded by so much
Having never felt so all alone
I stare upwards
At the stars of home

The strength of her hold
The power of her ties
Puts my head in my hands
And brings tears
To my eyes

Peering into the deep blue
Where it is only truth I see
Reflecting off this place

I know I should be

The Moon

Shooting the Moon, pardon the pun, Planets and Stars to obtain a line of position is done during morning or evening twilight. The time just before sunrise or just after sunset when the object becomes visible in the sky while still having enough light to illuminate the horizon.
The Moon can be used anytime it is visible during the day also.

The procedure used to obtain a line of position with these objects is the same as it is with the Sun with a few minor differences.

The Altitude Correction for the Moon is contained in its own table in the back of the Nautical Almanac.

The correction is done in two parts and is also contingent on whether the upper or lower limb of the Moon was observed.

Stars
by Chris Couch

It's the one I steer by
Through the dark of night
Shining above me as I sleep
Making my fairy tales
Come out right

A wish I make
Evening twilight fades
The first one I see
As the sky turns
It's darker shades

Floating on the edge
Of a galaxy we call home
Something in their twinkle
Tells us we are not alone

Gazing upwards
Searching near and far
Back through time
To whom we really are

Sailing towards the person
I am inside
The one overhead
That is my guide

Sprinkled by the dust
The stuff we are of
The stars of home
Peak through the clouds above

Mars, Venus, Saturn and Jupiter

Being some of the brightest objects in the night sky, the planets will be the last to disappear in the morning and the first to become visible in the evening.

Altitude corrections, GHA and Dec will all be found on the same pages as the Sun in the Nautical Almanac.

The Stars

Because the Stars remain fixed in their positions relative to each other, their location, SHA or Sidereal Hour Angle and Dec are listed for each day in the Nautical Almanac. GHA for a given Star is determined by adding GHA of Aries to the SHA of the Star. GHA Aries + SHA star = GHA of the Star

LHA is determined the same as the sun. GHA - Wlong or + Elong = LHA

The Night Sky

Look to the night sky. Find the prominent constellations, planets and brightest stars. Learn their names and how to locate them. With today's technology, it has never been easier. Two Apps I recommend are "Planets" and "Pocket Universe".

Imagine yourself alone on an open sea with nothing to guide you except the lights of the night sky.

Great Circle Sailing

The line between two points across the curved surface of our planet appears as a straight line. Take that curved surface and project it onto a flat surface as with a chart, and that straight line becomes a curve.

Seattle to Hawaii

For many hundreds of years it has been well known that the shortest distance between two points on the surface of our globe, is a great circle. It wasn't until the 1800's when point to point navigation became more accurate that we could take advantage of it.

Great Circle Calculator

This formula is used to determine the great circle distance initial course and intermediate points on a great circle route.

Distance:

- L1 = Departure Latitude
- L2 = Destination Latitude
- DLO = Difference in Longitude
- D = Distance

Notes:
1. If L1 and L2 are Contrary in name, Treat L2 as a negative.
2. If course is negative, add 180 degrees.
3. If DLO is greater than 180, enter as negative.
4. Distance in miles = = CosD x 60
5. Subtract when crossing the equator

Cos D = (Cos L1 x Cos L2 x Cos DLO) + -(Sin L1 x Sin L2)

Initial Course Angle:

$$\text{Cos Angle} = \frac{\text{Sin L2} - (\text{Cos Dist} \times \text{Sin L1})}{(\text{Sin Dist} \times \text{Cos L1})}$$

Note: Distance in degrees

Points along the route. Determine Lat for known Long.

- L1 = Departure Latitude
- L2 = Destination Latitude
- DLO1 = Diff of Dep Long to known Long
- DLO2 = Diff of Arrival Long to known Long
- DLO12 = Diff between Dep and Arr Long.

$$\text{Tan Lat} = \frac{\text{Tan L2} \times \text{Sin DLO1} = \text{Tan L1} \times \text{Sin SLO2}}{\text{Sin DLO12}}$$

So much more to the story...

When I first started to write this, my depth of knowledge as to our history was limited to what was already written in the history books.

But, in the past few years as I have researched further, it has become all too apparent that what we don't know about the sea going travels of our ancestors could fill volumes.

There is emerging evidence that over fifteen thousand years ago, during the last ice age, people's from Europe, followed the edge of the ice around the North Atlantic to the North American continent. These people later joined up with others who came from the west to become the Clovis people.

There is evidence that the Japanese landed on the west coast of South America. That the Polynesians landed on the west coast of the US.
The Phoenicians and then the Vikings landed on the east coast of North America.

All of this, thousands of years before Columbus and probably just the tip of the "History of Us" iceberg. It is certain, that on a planet that is covered mostly by water, our legacy is tied to the sea.

She *by Chris Couch*

Before me she lays
Old and wise
Her ancient hues
Reflect from my eyes

Sun shines when she laughs
Rain falls as tears
What is the hold she has had on me
All of these years

Humility has been taught
Respect she demands
Patience has been learned
I will obey her commands

I sail in her presence
She allows me in her world
I walk her laced edges
Her swells gently curled

Why am I drawn to her
This place from where we began
This force that humbles me so
I don´t know
I just am

I have known her fury
I have seen her wrath
Her beauty moves me

She is my path.

Our Connection

Boating for most of us is more than just recreation.
There is a sense of adventure, a fantasy, a dream.

We feel an inexplicable connection
to the water and to the sea.

Is it because that is where we come from?

Whether we are diving under it.
Swimming in it or floating on top
we feel like we are home.

Like this is the place we are meant to be.

Angel

by Chris Couch

*Graceful wings gentle breeze
Fills my sail unfurled
The way you guide my journey
The way you move my world*

*The subtle thoughts
I hear you say
The sound of your voice
That lights my way*

*Your angelic spirits
Watchful presence cast
Touches me softly
As I sail quietly past*

*Safe from the darkness
Drifting through oceans deep
Always by my side
Even as I sleep*

*A moon lit beach
With toes in the sand
You wrap your glow around me
And take me
By the hand*

*The tears that flow
When I am with you alone
Holding me tightly
As you carry me home*

Other Titles From Compass Headings Publishing...

The Checklist – A BOATER'S HANDBOOK
From Alaska to the Antilles, from Cabo to the Chesapeake.
40 pages, maintenance to maneuvering, trip planning to troubleshooting.

East Pacific Weather
—The West Coast weather can be very intimidating. This guide will break down the weather and trip planning into its component parts and then help you put the pieces back together into a plan you will understand and use. 52 pages.

www.CompassHeadingsPublishing.com

www.CompassHeadingsPublishing.com

www.ingramcontent.com/pod-product-compliance
Lightning Source LLC
LaVergne TN
LVHW071032070426
835507LV00003B/127